The FACT ATTACK series

FACT ATTACK

GRUESOME GHOSTS

IAN LOCKE

MACMILLAN CHILDREN'S BOOKS

First published 1998 by Macmillan Children's Books

This edition published 2012 by Macmillan Children's Books
a division of Macmillan Publishers Limited
20 New Wharf Road, London N1 9RR
Basingstoke and Oxford
Associated companies throughout the world
www.panmacmillan.com

ISBN 978-1-4472-2433-4

Text copyright © Ian Locke 1998
Illustrations copyright © Alan Rowe 1998

The right of Ian Locke and Alan Rowe to be identified as the
author and illustrator of this work has been asserted by them in
accordance with the Copyright, Designs and Patents Act 1988.

1 3 5 7 9 8 6 4 2

A CIP catalogue record for this book is available from
the British Library.

Printed and bound by CPI Group (UK) Ltd, Croydon CR0 4YY

DID YOU KNOW THAT . . .

Two ghosts have been seen at Marsham Tower, County Durham, which was built before 1314. One was of a woman and the other was of a pig.

At around ten o'clock on a May night in 1945, a Lancaster bomber with a Canadian crew smashed into the moors of the Peak District in the north of England and burst into flames, killing all the crew. Over fifty years later, in March 1997, a couple set out for a drive to see the Hale-Bopp comet. They ended up seeing something unbelievable – a strange plane flying towards them close to the ground. It seemed to be silent. A short distance away a gamekeeper and his wife heard an explosion and dashed outside. They could see an orange glow and a plume of smoke, as though a plane had crashed. A full-scale rescue was launched, but there was no trace of a crashed aircraft or fire and no plane had been reported missing. The sightings remained a mystery, but it seems possible that the ghost of the bomber had appeared in the night sky over the moors.

 In California the widow of the man who invented the Winchester Rifle had a house built with 13 flights of stairs, 13 bathrooms and 13 lights each with 13 bulbs. Each room had 13 bells and 13 locks. The house was built, she said, for the ghosts of all those killed by Winchester rifles. When she died in 1922 the house was left to the ghosts alone.

John Buckstone loved the Haymarket Theatre in London. Though he died in 1878 his ghost turns up in the dressing rooms of the theatre from time to time. He is said to only appear when things are going well.

 Huge hailstones fell in Venice, Italy, in 1906, killing many cats out on the city roofs.

 Linda Wade from Lancashire has a strange power – she is able to hear both sides of other people's telephone calls.

 A study in the United States once found that there were fewer people on trains which had accidents than those which didn't. This suggested that many people are somehow warned of accidents before they happen.

It is believed that no ghost can cross a flowing stream.

 Identical twins are often said to be able to contact each other by thought alone – or telepathy. In California, two twins once sat an exam. When their answers were looked at, it was found that they were almost exactly the same. Since there was no other way they could have been in touch with each other during the exam, some people thought they had used telepathy.

 Five films about or including ghosts:
1. *Ghostbusters*
2. *Caspar – The Friendly Ghost*
3. *Ghost*
4. *Blithe Spirit* (In this film by Sir Noel Coward, several ghosts appear.)
5. *Blackbeard's Ghost* (The ghost of the famous pirate.)

Deathbed visits of ghosts are common. When these ghosts appear, they bring peace, and are said to tell the person that someone is coming to take them away to another place.

 A person who claims to be able to communicate with those who have died is called a medium. In the 1980s the best-known British medium was Doris Stokes. She said she had a guardian spirit – an American Indian called Red Dawn. He first appeared in her bedroom and to prove he existed sent a "psychic wind" blowing through the room, which felt and looked just like a real wind.

 The ghost of a Second World War Wellington bomber has been seen flying down the Towy valley in Wales. It was completely silent.

Many people believe that they have lived previous lives. This is more common in Asia, where reincarnation is accepted. General Patton, the US general of the Second World War, believed he had been a Roman warrior.

 Glamis Castle, the home of the late Queen Mother, is haunted by the Tudor ghost of Lady Glamis who walks the castle gardens.

 A number of people have been said to be able to predict the future. Some have been very close to what actually happened: Robert Nixon, called the "Cheshire Idiot", foretold the English Civil War and the Great Fire of London over 100 years before they happened.

Mother Shipton of Yorkshire foretold the defeat of the Spanish Armada.

 Nostradamus, the famous French seer who died in 1566, wrote a book of his predictions, often known as Centuries. In the book he predicted the rise of Napoleon, the success of Louis Pasteur (the French chemist), the arrival of a dictator in Germany (except he called him Hister instead of Hitler), and the abdication of King Edward VIII of Britain.

 David Croly, an American who died in 1889, predicted the First World War, the arrival of cinema, multinational companies and air travel.

Count Hamon, a British clairvoyant, predicted the sinking of the *Titanic* and the death of the First World War British leader Lord Kitchener. In 1904, he very accurately predicted the murder of Rasputin in Russia. His other predictions included the Boer War, the First World War and a separate India and Pakistan.

Edgar Cayce, who died in 1945, was an American who seemed to be able to predict the future. He once said that California would split from the rest of the USA. He gave no date when this might happen, but, after his death, others said the date was April 1969. As a result there was panic in California during the month as people tried to leave the state – but nothing happened.

There are said to be more ghosts per square mile in Britain than in any other country.

Many people claim to have seen the phantom funeral train of President Lincoln of the USA, which is said to retrace the route of the original train of 1865 every year on the anniversary of President Lincoln's funeral.

 Often a Ouija board is used in seances – meetings which are said to conjure up spirits of the departed. The board was invented early in the century and called after the French and German words for "Yes" (*Oui* and *Ja*).

 The ghost of Anne Boleyn, the wife of Henry VIII, is said to return to Blickling Hall, Norfolk, each year on 19 May, the day she was executed in 1536. She sits in a coach pulled by four headless horses and driven by a headless coachman. She carries her own head on her knees. The coach drives up to the house and then disappears when it reaches the front door.

Many years ago, five people reported a "ghost train", with all its lights on, moving at high speed along a railway track in Sweden. It made no noise.

 In 1934 a man was killed in a car crash in London. It was found that he had died after the other driver swerved to avoid a bus in the road. The bus was a ghost! Though all lit up, it had no passengers or driver on board.

 Strange weather and falls from the sky have been recorded for centuries:

1. In 1847 a 50 kg block of ice fell over Ayrshire, Scotland. At the time there were no balloons, aeroplanes or other flying machines from which a block of ice could have fallen. Where the block of ice came from remains a mystery.

2. During the Second World War there was a shower of frogs over Alton Towers, the big house in Staffordshire, for an hour and a half.

3. On a bright June day in 1948, Ian Pate, at Barton on Sea, near Bournemouth, saw fish falling from the sky. They covered 100 metres. There was not a cloud in the sky.

4. A shower of hazelnuts fell from a clear blue sky in March near Westbury Park in Bristol in March 1977.

5. Insect eggs in jelly fell from the sky at Eton, Berkshire, in midsummer, 1911.

6. Rain fell from a clear sky at Grayshott, Hampshire, in 1929, 1931 and 1933.

7. Frogs fell from the sky near Whittington military barracks, Staffordshire, in September 1956.

8. It rained pennies and halfpennies at Hanham in Avon in September 1956.

9. Eggs fell from the sky at Wokingham in Berkshire in December 1974.

10. In July 1888 rain was reported falling from a clear sky at Stevenage in Hertfordshire.

 Art teacher Austin Hepburn took pictures of what may have been the Loch Ness monster in August 1996. The photos show an unexplained movement in the otherwise dead calm water, which lasted about four minutes.

A woman had a dream about a horse race in 1949. She somehow knew the race she saw in her dream was the Derby, which was due to be run the next day. When she woke she could remember clues about the horses that finished in her dream. She looked at the morning paper and looked at the list of the runners for the Derby. She picked out three horses from the list and wrote them down. She asked her husband to put bets on them as he went to work. In the Derby the horses finished in the order she had written them and she won all her bets.

 While there have been ghost trains, a ghost lift is unusual! When the Palace Hotel in Southport on Merseyside was being demolished in 1969, the lift took on a life of its own. Even when all the power was off, the lift moved – its doors opened and closed, its lights flashed and it went up and down. What was even odder was that the brake for the lift was on – so it shouldn't have moved at all!

The ghost of Catherine Howard, one of the wives of Henry VIII, is heard as shrieks in the haunted gallery of Hampton Court Palace; she is heard running along the gallery and into the chapel at the end. She was beheaded on February 13 1542.

 When Donald Campbell of England set the world land speed record of 403.1 mph at Lake Eyre in 1964, he said he saw the face of his dead father in his windscreen. His father said to him, "Don't worry, it'll be all right, boy."

 A monster was seen on a lake at the edge of a forest in Java in 1975. It was said to be a six-metre-long prehistoric monster. It looked like a giant fish or turtle. Local fishermen burned opium on the lake to keep the monster happy.

King Charles I arrived at Northampton in 1645, prepared to do battle with Oliver Cromwell's army the next day. He stayed at the Wheatsheaf hotel in the town. During the night he was visited by the ghost of Lord Stafford, his friend and adviser, who had been killed early in the Civil War. The ghost twice told Charles he should leave Northampton and take his army north. The king decided to do what the ghost told him, frightened by what might happen if he did not take the advice. However, Charles's generals persuaded him to stay and the battle was fought at Naseby on June 14. In the battle the King's forces suffered a heavy defeat. The Cavaliers never recovered from this battle and Charles ended up losing everything, finally being executed in London.

A three-masted ship, the *Marion G. Douglas*, was found off the Isles of Scilly, near Cornwall, in 1919. She was in perfect condition. Her boats and her motorboat were still on board. The cargo of timber had not been moved. Everything seemed normal, except that none of the crew could be found!

The only British Prime Minister to be assassinated was Spencer Perceval. He dreamed of the event on May 10 1812. The next morning he told his dream to his family and friends. They tried to persuade him not to go to the House of Commons that day, but he went all the same. Things turned out as he had seen in his dream.

During the summer of 1808, a clergyman, Mr McLean, was out in a boat off the small island of Coll, near the coast of Scotland. Several other boats were not far away as he went out to sea. A little way from the shore he noticed what looked like a rock. As he went closer he saw it move and then got the fright of his life. The head of a creature with yellow eyes and a long neck came out of the water. Scared stiff, Mr McLean headed for the shore. There he landed and watched the creature from the sand. He and the others nearby all said it was an unknown monster some 25 metres long.

Among the famous ghosts in stories is that of Marley. The ghost of Jacob Marley appears in Charles Dickens's *A Christmas Carol*.

Four kings and queens are said to haunt
Windsor Castle, including Elizabeth I.

Poltergeists are said to be spirits which
are able to move things and make
noises. They are mostly harmless.
A poltergeist was found in a Welsh
farmhouse in 1904. It threw all sorts
of things around, moved pictures,
dropped crockery, mixed up food
and wrote little messages all over the
house. One night ten people, including
a policeman, sat up to watch for this
spirit. After a time it arrived. The first
thing it did was pick up a lump of
butter and throw it into the face of the
policeman!

Days before he was assassinated, US
President Abraham Lincoln had a dream
about the event, and told his wife about it
the next morning.

A woman who said she could predict the end of the world was arrested in Finland in 1923. She had said it was useless to own land, to save money or do any work. A lot of people who believed her were left ruined.

One night during the First World War in 1915, a young Adolf Hitler was serving in the German Army in the trenches. At dinner time, he was sitting down when he heard a voice which told him to move twenty metres. He did so. As soon as he sat down again, a shell hit the part of the trench he had just left. Everyone was killed. Hitler took the strange warning to be a great omen for his future.

Shortly after the Second World War broke
out, a bus driver, a Mr Nott, took his bus
across the open country of Exmoor in
Devon on Christmas Eve. There were only
two passengers and the conductor on
board. As Mr Nott reached a place called
Blackmoor Gate he was amazed to see an
enormous dog and two sheep appear in the
road ahead of the bus. Though he braked
hard, the driver knew he was going to hit
them and braced himself for the shock. But
the shock never came. As soon as the bus
stopped, Mr Nott leaped out. There was
nothing on the road. One of the passengers
had also seen the animals and he was
equally mystified by their disappearance.
They could only have been ghosts.

A hum haunted the house of the Binkowskis in Rotterdam, New York, in the early 1960s. Experts investigated the house but could find no cause for this constant low noise. As the hum continued, the family fell ill. The odd noise was talked about and hundreds of people visited the house and also heard it. No effort was spared to try and find its cause, but with no result. Eventually, after nine months, the family moved into the garage.

 One of the most haunted houses in London was 50 Berkeley Square – it is now the home of the well-known rare book dealers Maggs Brothers.

 The Swedish writer Swedenborg arrived at the port of Gothenburg in Sweden in September 1759. He went to have dinner with an English friend in the town. During the meal he suddenly turned very pale and announced that fire was sweeping through the Swedish capital Stockholm – 480 km away. Upset by his vision he left the house, coming back only a short time later to say that the fire was now under control and had stopped only three doors from his own home. The next evening a courier was able to confirm that everything had happened as Swedenborg had described!

 In Somerset, toast is dipped in cider and hung on apple trees to drive off evil spirits.

 On a clear December day a ship, the *Dei Gratia*, was sailing across the Atlantic when another vessel, with two sails set, was sighted in the distance. As the *Dei Gratia* moved closer, no one could be seen on the deck of the other ship. Three men were sent over to examine the seemingly deserted vessel. As they approached the desolate ship, they found it was the *Mary Celeste*, which had sailed out of New York. As they clambered aboard, the three called out for anyone – there was no reply. The ship's boat was missing. They searched the ship and there was no one on board, though the captain's bed was unmade, the pots and pans in the galley were all in place, and everything else seemed in order. The only strange thing was a dampness throughout the ship. Reaching the cargo of alcohol, they found it all in place. The crew of the *Dei Gratia* were mystified by the state of the ship. A skeleton crew was ordered to take the ship in hand and sail it to the Azores. What happened to the *Mary Celeste* remains a mystery. It was obvious that all aboard had taken to the boat, but no trace of them was ever found.

A prison doctor, Ernest Helby, was riding his motorbike on a road across Dartmoor, the desolate moorland in Devon, in 1921. In his sidecar he carried his two children. Suddenly he told them to jump out. The motorbike swerved off the road and the doctor was killed in the crash. The children survived and later said they had seen a pair of ghostly hairy hands on the handlebars just before the crash. About eight weeks later, a young army officer was thrown from his motorbike on the same road. Afterwards he explained that he had seen a pair of hairy hands appear over his own and he lost control of the bike. The hands are said to be those of an Italian who worked at a nearby gunpowder factory. One day, after drinking, he went into the factory and forgot to take off his boots. The boots had nails in their soles and made a spark. The explosion blew the man to bits.

During a very cold snowy winter in 1855, Albert Brailsford, head of the village school at Topsham, Devon, discovered a trail of unusual hoofprints in the snow outside his front door. He found the prints were all over the place, even on rooftops! Other reports of the strange hoofprints came in and it was found that they stretched over 40 miles. They remained a mystery and became known as "the Devil's footprints".

 A red ghost appeared to Henry IV of France in 1610, predicting his death the next day. The same ghost was seen by the bed of the French Emperor Napoleon by his doctor on 5 May 1821, just before Napoleon died.

 Littledean Hall in Gloucestershire has a host of ghosts, including Civil War Cavalier soldiers, a monk and an 18th-century servant who was murdered by his master.

The yeti, or abominable snowman, said to be part man, part creature, was first seen in the high mountains of India as long ago as 1832, by the British explorer B. H. Hodgson.

 A dream once saved a king. In 1912 a man named Saracini was in an Italian jail. He had been sent to prison in 1880 for the murder of a man on a road. (Strangely, though the man had been killed by a kick from Saracini's mule, it was Saracini who was found guilty by the court.) One night Saracini had a strange dream. He dreamt he saw an attempt to kill the King and Queen of Italy. Waking up, he told his dream in detail to the warder. The story was told to the chief of police, and, because of the details in Saracini's dream, the police were told to take extra care. As a result of this care,

an assassin was held after he fired three
shots at the king and queen, but missed.
Though Saracini had saved the King and
Queen through his dream, he was left
in prison until 1926, when the new King
heard about his dream and ordered a
new trial. This time the mule was found
guilty of murder and Saracini was freed.

 The most well-known picture of
the Loch Ness monster, with its
neck out of the water, was taken
by London surgeon Robert Wilson
in April 1934. The famous photo
was, it seems, made up from a toy
submarine and a model head on top
and was exposed as a fake in 1994.

The Israeli Uri Geller became famous in the 1970s for his apparent ability to bend spoons, forks and other metal objects by thought and rubbing alone. When he was showing what he could do on TV, thousands of people rang or sent in letters to the TV stations saying that their spoons and forks had also been bent while Mr Geller was on TV. Though some people did not believe that Mr Geller could bend metal without using some sort of trick, he did seem to have some strange power. In the 1980s a man in Britain was hunting for the wreck of a submarine, but could not find it. In the end, by chance, he was able to see Uri Geller and asked him if he knew where it was. Geller pointed to a spot and said that was where the missing sub would be found. About ten years later, the search for the lost sub was restarted. Believe it or not, it was found exactly where Uri Geller said it would be found!

Throughout 1996, there were many
protestors at the place where a new
road, the Newbury by-pass, was to be
built in southern England. The planned
route would cause the destruction
of woodland and that meant many
animals would lose their homes. By
the end of the summer the last of the
protestors had left and the security
guards thought they would be left in
peace. However, in December, some
of the guards became very frightened
by the unexpected. They saw the
ghosts of Roundhead and Cavalier
soldiers who had fought the battle of
Newbury on that spot during the Civil
War over three hundred and fifty years
before!

The ghost of Anne Boleyn, the second wife of Henry VIII, who was beheaded, moves around a bit. She has been seen at the White Tower at the Tower of London and in the chapel of St Peter in Chains Church, London, where she is buried. In 1864 a soldier at the Tower of London was arrested and court-martialled because he was unconscious at his post. In court, the man explained he had fallen into a faint and knocked himself out after seeing the ghost of Anne Boleyn in the Tower. The ghost has been seen as a shape or as a clear ghost figure, carrying her head under her arm!

 People in a house in West Yorkshire were terrified by a pair of gloves. The gloves appeared at the bottom and top of the doors, like a gruesome pair of hands! When an aunt in the room began to sing a hymn to get rid of the spirit, the gloves began to tap out the time of the hymn.

The writer C. S. Lewis, famous for *The Chronicles of Narnia*, had many friends and many people he wrote to. A few days after he died in 1963 one of the friends was sitting watching television one evening when C. S. Lewis suddenly appeared, sitting in a chair close by, and spoke to the friend. The apparition had a redder face than normal, but otherwise looked quite well. Having said a few words which helped the friend with a problem, he disappeared. A week later, while the friend was reading in bed, just before going to sleep, Lewis appeared again, repeating the words of a few days before. And again, he disappeared.

 The first sighting of a large ape-like creature in the forests of North America was in the 19th century. The creature became known as Bigfoot, after David Thompson found very large footprints of an unknown creature in Canada. Bigfoot was filmed in colour by Roger Patterson on October 20 1967. He was some way away, but the pictures from the 10 metres of film show an ape-like creature moving fairly fast among the trees of the forest. The footprints found afterwards were 16 inches long and 7 inches across.

 There are several ghosts at the Houses of Parliament. A woman in pink has been seen at the west front of the House of Lords, where the Palace of Westminster used to be. Another of the ghosts is a man in black seen wandering the galleries from time to time.

 The ghost of the first wife of the British poet Shelley, who died about 150 years ago, has been seen in Hyde Park, London. She drowned herself in the lake in the park, the Serpentine.

An unusual ghost was seen in the library of the York Museum in late 1953. The caretaker was checking through the building as usual when he came across a man still there. He seemed to be looking for a book. What was odd was his clothes – he had on an old-fashioned frock coat, thin trousers and elastic-sided boots. As the caretaker came nearer, he heard the man say, "I must find it. I must find it!" When he reached out to touch the man, the figure disappeared, dropping a book as he went. The ghost has been seen or heard by several other people, and each time the same book dropped to the floor.

 Some 17 miles out in the Atlantic ocean, off Scotland, lie the Flannan Isles. On one of the islands a lighthouse was built, opening at the end of 1899. Three men, James Ducat, Donald McArthur and Thomas Marshall, went out to the island as lighthouse-keepers. During a wild storm eleven days before Christmas the following year, the light suddenly went out. Once the storm had passed, a ship set out for the island on Boxing Day to find out what had happened. The island and lighthouse were empty! In the lighthouse, the beds were made and all was tidy. The last entry in the records was on 15 December; everything seemed to be in order. Yet, for some unknown reason, the three men had disappeared without trace. While there were all sorts of theories about what happened, no sign of the men was ever found.

 The Loch Ness monster was first sighted in about AD 565 when St Columba is said to have driven the monster away from a swimmer in the loch.

In March 1939, about 60 people at Glencairn beach, South Africa, saw the ghost of a fully rigged ship moving towards the sands. The sails were all set for a storm, but there was not a breath of wind. As the crowd looked on, the "phantom" ship disappeared.

 The ghost of Major W. H. Braddell, who had been killed by a German bomb in 1941, was seen in the Egremont room of the Naval and Military Club in London in March 1994.

 During the plague in London in 1665, flaming swords, coffins, ghosts and angels were seen over the city.

The biggest gunfight in the history of the FBI took place against a woman gangster, Ma Barker, and her gang in a house in the country in the USA. Ma and her gang were all killed in the shoot-out. Years later, the ghost of Ma, combing her hair, was seen sitting on the end of a bed in the house. Downstairs the sound of "her boys" playing cards was heard. When a guest in the house went to look there was no one there.

 After 1931, the flat above the David Belasco Theater in New York was left empty after the theatre owner died. Late at night stagehands said they heard David Belasco's private lift begin to start. It clanked as it moved upstairs – there could be no doubt about the sound. Upstairs there was no sign of the ghost. One of the managers later said he could feel the presence of Belasco in his office.

A haunted house in the north of Britain once had a ghost who appeared when his relatives put his photo away. He only disappeared after his photo was put back on display.

 Jeane Dixon, an American woman who died in 1997, seemed to be able to see the future. She accurately predicted the death of President Roosevelt in 1945 and the assassination of President Kennedy in 1963. She was not right all the time – she predicted a third World War in 1958 and that a Russian would be the first man on the moon.

 The earliest poltergeist was seen in Italy over 1,400 years ago.

A ghost is said to haunt the Drury Lane Theatre, London. It is the figure of a young man who was murdered there in 1780. To see him is said to bring success. The skeleton of the man was found by workmen early in the last century, entombed in a wall. There were still the shreds of a grey riding coat covering the skeleton, and a dagger was sticking out of the ribs.

 In 1918 a Russian huntsman told the French consul in Vladivostock, on the tip of the Siberian wilderness, that years ago he had tracked "chestnut-coloured elephants" in the forest. He said he had seen their tracks and followed them. After several days he caught sight of one of the animals. What he described was a mammoth, covered with shaggy hair. The only problem is that mammoths died out thousands of years ago!

In a broken-down house in Hydesville, New York state, America, there lived a poor Canadian, John D. Fox. He had three children. One March morning in 1848, the children heard knocks and raps in the house. The noises went on for days, until the noise and movement was so strong that the old house shook. One of the girls, Catherine, aged 7, clapped to answer the knocks. Almost at once a clap answered. Next she snapped her fingers. Again, the sound came back. Her sister Margaret, aged 10, joined in and again there was an answer. Margaret went to get her parents and showed them what happened. The amazed mother and father began to work out a way to "talk" to the ghost by knocks – and it answered! The spirit said it was the ghost of Charles Rosma, a peddler who had been murdered there. The story of the haunted house became so well known in America that the two sisters toured the country.

Loch Ness is the largest British lake; it is 22 miles (35 km) long, almost a mile (1.5 km) wide and 950 feet (264 metres) deep.

 The ghost of Abraham Lincoln, the president of the United States who was assassinated by John Wilkes Booth in 1865, haunts the White House in Washington. About 60 years ago a maid saw his ghost sitting on the edge of a bed, taking off his shoes. In 1945 Lincoln's ghost was seen by the Dutch queen Wilhelmina, while she was staying at the White House.

 During the First World War a German submarine, the U-65, which had had some unexplained accidents since it was built, was in Bruges in Belgium. It was to take on fuel and arms. A torpedo warhead was being loaded when it blew up, killing 11 people, including the second lieutenant. As the crippled sub was being towed to a dry dock for repair, a crewman left, saying he'd seen the dead officer standing at the head of the ship with his arms folded. Just before the U-65 sailed, another crewman deserted, saying he'd also seen the ghost. Even when the sub got going, sightings of the ghost continued. When the ship returned to base, the captain was killed, and because of its reputation a chaplain was called to exorcise the ship. The bad luck continued: a gunner went mad, the chief engineer broke his leg and another crewman killed himself. Finally, on the morning of July 10 1918, off Cape Clear in Ireland, the U-65 was seen by a US submarine, the L-2. The US submarine was about to open fire when a huge explosion ripped through the German U-boat and she sank with all hands. What caused the explosion will never be known.

On 4 August 1951, two English sisters-in-law were staying at Puys, a seaside village near Dieppe on the north French coast. They were awoken in the very early morning by men shouting. These sounds were followed by the sound of gunfire and aeroplanes at about four in the morning. They looked out, but could see nothing. They could not explain what happened. The noises of battle continued for almost three hours, until there was silence at about seven in the morning. It is thought that the women had heard a ghost battle. It was the battle that took place at Dieppe some seven years before.

 It is not what you expect at work. The ghost of the 4th Duke of Norfolk used to wander about Coutts Bank in London. He'd been beheaded for treason in 1512. Receptionists saw the headless ghost wandering about, dressed in Elizabethan clothes.

The most common feeling when ghosts appear is that the air goes very chilly.

 Each year, the ghosts of two young women in Victorian dress have been seen at the Albert Hall, London. In the spring of 1996 a ghostbuster was called in to see if they could be made to go away.

 Sir Arthur Conan Doyle, the creator of Sherlock Holmes, spent many years investigating ghosts and the unexplained.

 The book *Elvis is Alive*, written by Gail Brewer Giorgio, became a bestseller in the USA in 1988. In 1996 it was said that the FBI had a photo of Elvis taken in 1982, five years after he died.

Margaret Sheridan came across a ghost when she was about 17 at her family house in Frampton, England. At the time her father was in France, fighting in the First World War. Margaret was coming down the stairs for tea one day when she saw a boy on the stairs. He wore a white sailor suit and a straw hat on his head. He was about her age. The two looked at each other, but did not speak as they passed each other. Margaret thought the stranger was a guest. She went in to tea and told everyone there she had seen the boy in the sailor's costume on the stairs. No one spoke. Later, Margaret found out that the boy was the ghost of an ancestor who had died at sea. He would appear in the house when the heir to the Sheridan family was about to die. A few days later a letter arrived saying that Margaret's father had been killed in the war.

The Society for Psychical Research is a group which looks into stories of ghosts and other strange things. It was formed over 100 years ago.

 In 1992, 50 years after the Battle of Britain, on a clear warm summer's day, just as it had been for the battle, visitors to a Battle of Britain museum in Kent had a strange sensation. They felt as though some of the airmen who had fought and died in the battle were looking over their shoulders as they examined the exhibits.

 Exotic creatures often turn up in odd places – a New Guinea fruit bat, with a one-metre wingspan, was found clinging to a car in Exeter, Devon, on October 3 1984. Where it came from was a mystery.

On a walk in Austria, the writer Barbara Cartland and her brother came across a fairy-tale castle. When they told villagers about this marvellous building, they were astonished to be told that the castle had been destroyed years before.

For some time in the 1980s it was hard to get people to move into houses in the Northwest Territories in Canada. The problem did not go away. The government tried to find out why, and got a very strange answer. They found that many of the houses were said to be haunted. No one wanted to live in a house with a ghost. A local councillor said the government should hire an exorcist to drive the spirits away!

In 1977 and 1978 a poltergeist seemed to be throwing food around in a house in Derbyshire. Black pudding, eggs, bacon, bread, tomatoes and even a joint of beef flew through the air for no reason. The throwing happened every other night. Sometimes the spirit would stop for weeks, then start again. The poltergeist only disappeared after police came to the house.

In 1973 a primary school head teacher in Wales was driving home at night. As he approached an old railway bridge, a young girl stepped from the hedge in front of his car. He braked quickly. But nothing happened. The headmaster was sure he saw the girl's face come closer and closer then pass through the car. When he told his scary story, other people came forward to say they had had the same frightening experience.

In 1974 a US expedition to Loch Ness took photos under the water. When enhanced by computer, the pictures seemed to show a large body with a long neck and flippers. On this evidence, the American Academy said that there was a "large unknown creature in the waters of Loch Ness".

 During the 1940s, stories came from Kenya, Africa, about a "bear" which roamed the country. It was said to attack and kill goats and people. A hunter went to search for the creature in Kenya. Early one morning, with mist rising from the ground, he was called from his tent by his helper. Outside, he was able to see a red-coloured animal ahead. It was about 2.5 metres tall and stood on its back legs. After a short time it dropped down into the tall grass, then stood up again a little later. The hunter tried to shoot the creature, so it could be caught, but his shot missed. He was sure the creature was unknown. The next day he was told that this creature had gone into a native hut and killed and partly eaten a woman there.

 When Mrs Lincoln, the wife of President Lincoln, had her photo taken after the President had died, the photograph included a ghostly image of the President.

 At least four skulls which are said to scream if anyone tries to bury them are kept in Britain.

When making a record-breaking row across the Atlantic with Chay Blythe in 1966, Captain John Ridgway saw a sea monster at least 10 metres long, which glowed at the edges. The captain had seen all sorts of sea creatures during his life, but nothing like this.

 The ghost of a Daimler car was seen from July 1964 to September 1975 on a road in Devon.

 The first photo of a "spirit" was said to have been taken by William Mumler in the USA. When he developed a photo of himself sitting in a chair for a self-portrait, the ghost image of a young girl appeared on his knee.

The most haunted house in Britain was probably Borley Rectory in Essex. This large house had been strange for years and no one wanted to live in it for very long. In 1939 a new owner moved in. While he was unpacking, an oil lamp overturned for no reason and set the house on fire. The owner escaped the blaze and joined a small crowd outside. Two figures, a man and a woman, were seen leaving the burning house, but disappeared. The house was left a burned-out shell, with no one in it. Yet at least one man heard sounds around it, including thundering horses' hooves. During the war lights were reported at the house. But there was never anything there. Four years after the fire, the house was knocked down. The ground was searched. About a metre underground workmen found the remains of a woman's skull and a small collection of jewellery.

At Beverley in Yorkshire a video was taken of the rooms in an empty house. When the film was played back, the image of a girl appeared. She was believed to be the ghost of a maid who had killed herself in the house.

A ghost was photographed at Combermere Hall in Cheshire in 1891.

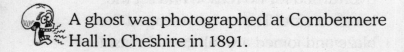

In 1928 an elephant-keeper at London Zoo was murdered while asleep. His fellow keeper was found guilty and hanged for the murder. The ghost of the keeper, Ali, haunts the zoo. In the mammal house a strange humming is sometimes heard. The mammal house was built over the old elephant house in 1967. Ali is said to still stalk the place at night.

On a winter's night, after a long day at work, Dr Mitchell of Philadelphia in the USA heard his doorbell ring. Opening the door, he saw a small girl. She said her mother was very sick and could he come at once. She would show him the way. The doctor followed the girl. He found the woman very ill and at once gave her medicine to help her get better. As he was leaving the room, the doctor remarked that the woman was lucky to have such a helpful daughter. The woman was very surprised. She told the doctor that her daughter had died about a month before!

The writer Robert Graves met a young
man called Challoner when the two went
to train for the army. They were to be
together until Challoner was sent off to
France to fight in the First World War.
As he left, Challoner shook hands with
Graves, saying, "I'll meet you again in
France, sir." Months later Challoner was
killed without meeting Graves again. In
June that year, Graves was out in France
with the army. One evening, while he
and his men were having a special
dinner to celebrate their safe return from
the fighting, Graves noticed a familiar
face through the window of the house.
Challoner was looking in at him. The
ghost saluted, then went on his way.
Graves jumped up and looked out of
the window. He could see no sign of the
ghost.

A man was out walking on a visit to an area he did not know in Australia when he came across a collection of buildings and heard water gushing nearby. On his return he told his father about the place he had seen. His father was curious and went out to the spot. But there was nothing there. Years later he learned the place his son had seen had once existed (it had been built for miners) but had not been around for almost 100 years.

 British boxer Michael Jones, who had just seen the film *Fear*, was bitten on the neck by a complete stranger outside a cinema in Swindon. The cinema was also showing *Dracula: Dead and Loving It*!